LOOK! LOOK! the Giggle BOOK

Look out for
THAT PEST JONATHAN
also by William Cole and Tomi Ungerer
published by The O'Brien Press

Collected by
WILLIAM COLE

LOOK! LOOK! the Giggle BOOK

Pictures by
TOMI UNGERER

The O'Brien Press
DUBLIN

This revised and redesigned edition first published 1994
by The O'Brien Press Ltd., 20 Victoria Road, Rathgar, Dublin 6, Ireland.
First published 19867, Reprinted 1970, 1980.

Copyright © William Cole and Tomi Ungerer

All rights reserved. No part of this book may be reproduced or utilised in any way or by any means, electronic or mechanical, including photocopying, recording or by any information storage and retrieval system without permission in writing from the publisher. This book may not be sold as a bargain book or at a reduced rate without permission in writing from the publisher.

The author and publisher thank the following for permission to reproduce poems in this book: Ian Serraillier and Oxford University Press for 'Too Polite' from *Happily Ever After* 1963; Shel Silverstein c/o William Cole for 'A wonderful thing . . .' and 'Oh, who will wash'; Pyke Johnson, Jr., for 'Toucan'; Spike Milligan Productions Ltd., for 'Tell Me Little Woodworm' from *Silly Verse for Kids* by Spike Milligan.

British Library cataloguing-in-publication Data
A catalogue reference for this title is available from the British Library.

ISBN 0-86278-367-4

10 9 8 7 6 5 4 3 2 1

Cover illustration: Tomi Ungerer
Cover design: Neasa Ní Chianáin
Separations (cover): Lithoset Ltd., Dublin;
Separations (internal drawings): Irish Photo Ltd., Dublin
Printing: Cox & Wyman Ltd., Reading

Limerick Giggles

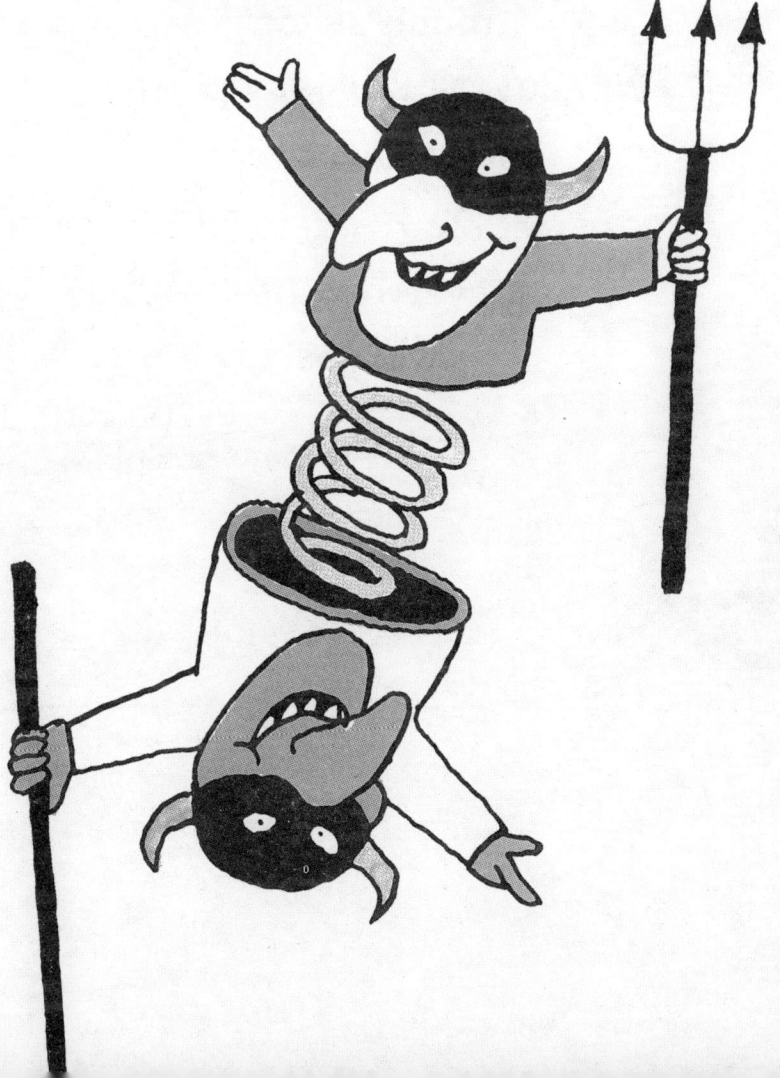

Said the lion, 'There's so
much *space*,
Whenever I walk any place –
*I never would say
"Get out o' my way!"* –
But everyone does –
just in case.'

WILLIAM COLE

Poor Phoebe P. Peabody Sutter –
Letter B always caused her to stutter:
'Give me,' she said,
'Some buh-buh-buh-bread,
And buh-buh-buh-buh-buh-buh-butter.'

Here is a very strange man,
Who lives in Japan in a can;
His favourite thrill
Is to roll down the hill,
Again and again and again!

                         WILLIAM COLE

I raised a great hullabaloo
When I found a big mouse
in my stew;
Said the waiter, 'Don't shout
And wave it about
Or the rest will be wanting one,
too!'

A sleeper from the Amazon
Put nighties of his gra'mazon –
    The reason? That
    He was too fat
To get his own pajamazon.

There was a young lady of Spain,
Who couldn't go out in the rain,
'Cause she'd lent her umbrella
To Queen Isabella,
Who never returned it again.

There was a small maiden
 named Maggie,
Whose dog was enormous and
 shaggy;
   The front end of him
   Looked vicious and grim –
But the tail end was friendly and
 waggy.

There was a young lady
of Woosester
Who usest to crow like
a roosester,
She usest to climb
Two trees at a time
But her sisester usest to
boosest her.

There was a fat fellow from Rye,
Who plunged in the ocean, and
  my!
    The tide had been out
    But he was so stout
He changed the low tide into
  high!

WILLIAM COLE

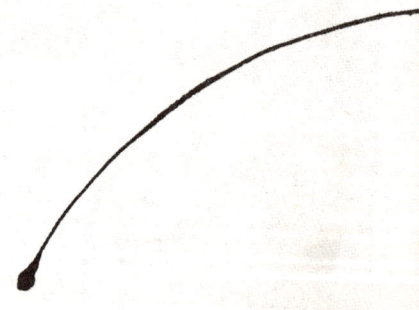

'Mommy! Mommy! All the kids at school say I look like a monkey!'
'Oh, now don't worry about it, darling, just go upstairs and comb your face.'

'O.K., smarty. What's six and four?'

'Eleven.'

'Nah! Six and four's ten!'

'Couldn't be. *Five and five's ten!*'

'Oh, Sir, did you miss
your train?'
'Not at all. I didn't like its
looks, so
I chased it out of the station.'

'I wish I had enough money to buy a hippopotamus.'
'A hippo*pot*amus? What do you want a hippopotamus for?'
'I don't. I just want the money.'

First Twin: 'Wow, it's cold! My feet are frozen and they're sticking out of the covers!'
Second Twin: 'Well, for goodness' sakes, pull them in.'
First Twin: 'Oh, no! I'm not putting those cold things in bed with me!'

'Hello. Is this number one-one-one-one?'
'No. This is eleven-eleven.'
'Oh. Sorry to have bothered you.'
'That's O.K. I had to get up anyway to answer the phone.'

'Do you have holes in your underwear?'
'Of course I don't have holes in my underwear!'
'Then how do you get your feet through?'

'I always make a game out of taking a bath.'
'How interesting. What do you call it?'
'Ring around the bathtub.'

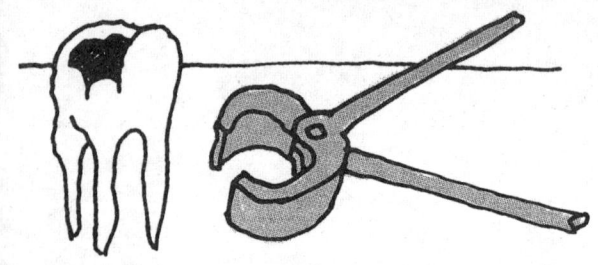

DENTIST: 'My, this is the largest cavity I've ever seen ... I've ever seen ...'
PATIENT: 'You needn't repeat yourself, Doctor.'
DENTIST: 'I didn't. That was an echo ... an echo ...'

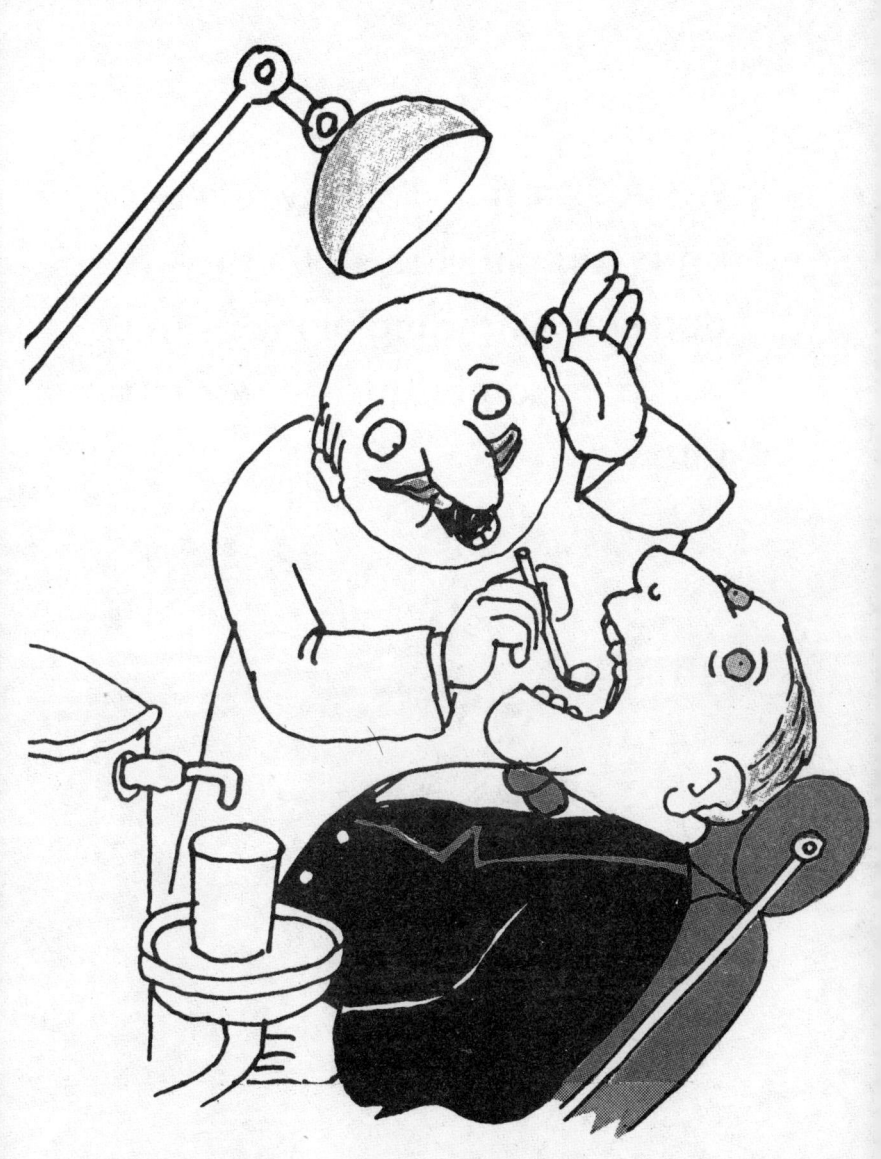

FATHER: 'Darn it, Tommy, every time you play the violin the dog starts howling along. Can't you play some tune he doesn't know?'

'My father and I together – we know everything in the world.'
'Yeah? What's the square root of 144?'
'That's one my father knows.'

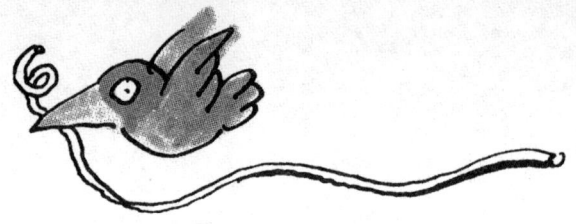

A wonderful thing happened to
  my sister Lettie, it did;
Instead of hair, she grew a lot of
  spaghetti, she did.
And now whenever she wants a
  snack at night, she does,
She simply combs it down and
  takes a bite, she does.

                                      SHEL SILVERSTEIN

Here is Charles Augustus Brown;
He's a very funny clown!
Now ask him why he wears a
 frown.
 He'll say, 'You've got me upside down!'

> WILLIAM COLE

The Toucan

Of all the birds I know, few can
Boast of as large a bill as the
  toucan.
Yet I can think of one who can,
And if you think a while, too,
  you can:
Another toucan
In the zoo can.

PYKE JOHNSON, JR.

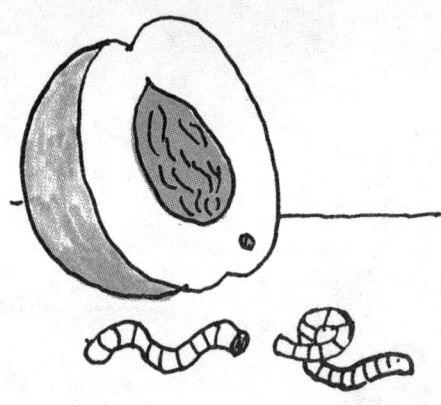

It's such a shock, I almost screech,
When I find a worm inside my peach!
But then, what *really* makes me blue,
Is to find a worm who's bit in two!

WILLIAM COLE

Uncle Nat
Is short and fat
When he signs his name
It looks like that

And Uncle Jim
Is tall and slim
And when *he* writes
it looks like *him*

Too Polite

Broad met Stout
At the gate, and each
Was too polite to brush past.
'After you!' said Broad.
'After you!' said Stout.
They got in a dither
And went through together
And both
      STUCK
         FAST.

IAN SERRAILLIER

If I was a farmer, I'd have an
 easy time;
I'd pick the nice red apples
 from the nice red-apple vine;
I'd pick delicious watermelons
 from the watermelon tree,
And oh, how lazy-happy I would
 be!

American Folk Rhyme

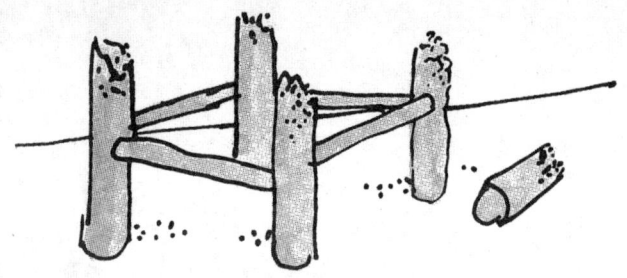

Tell me little woodworm
Eating thru the wood.
Surely all that sawdust
Can't do you any good.

Heavens! Little woodworm
You've eaten all the chairs
So that's why poor old
  Grandad's
Sitting outside on the stairs.

SPIKE MILLIGAN

My breakfast was ice cream
With pickles sliced in it;
My lunch, three fat pork chops
Chewed up in one minute;
For dinner, some orange pop
And liverwurst, sliced thick –
And now, please excuse me,
It's time to be sick!

WILLIAM COLE

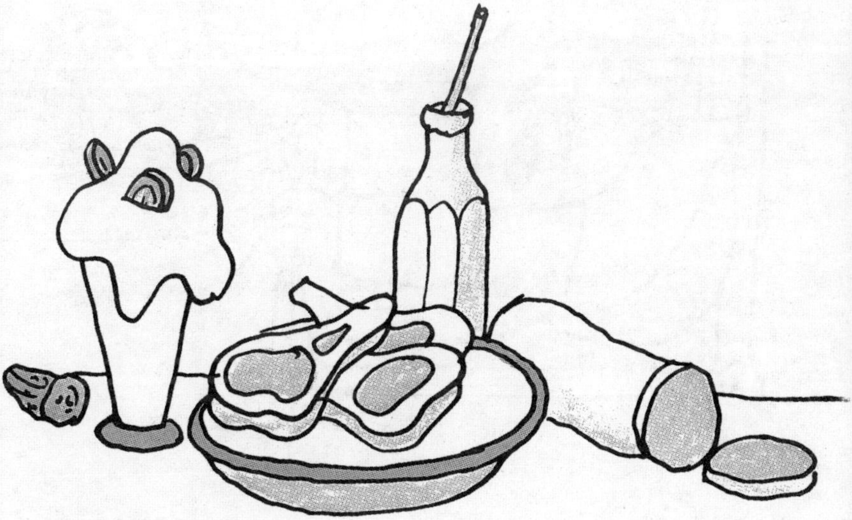

Get up, get up, you sleepyhead,
Get up you lazy sinner;
We need those sheets for tablecloths –
It's nearly time for dinner.

Oh, who will wash the tiger's ears?
And who will comb his tail?
And who will brush his sharp white teeth?
And who will file his nails?

Oh, Bobby may wash the tiger's ears
and Susy may file his nails
and Lucy may brush his long white teeth
and I'll go down for the mail.

SHEL SILVERSTEIN

Whatever's become
Of poor Tom Thumb?
He's *disappeared*
In his bubble gum!

                    WILLIAM COLE

Forth from his den to steal he stole,
His bags of chink he chunk,
And many a wicked smile he smole,
And many a wink he wunk.

I love to go to lectures,
And make the audience stare,
By walking 'round upon
their heads,
And spoiling people's hair!

GELETT BURGESS

A Rash of Riddles

Why is a lion in the desert like Christmas?

Because of his sandy claws.

What did the big firecracker say to the little firecracker?

My pop's bigger 'n your pop!

What did the mother ghost say to the baby ghost?

Fasten your sheet belt.

What has a neck but no head?

A bottle.

Why is it hard for a leopard to hide in the jungle?

'Cause he's always spotted.

What did the ground say to the rain?
If you keep this up, my name will be mud.

What became of that guy who stole the calendar?
He got twelve months.

What's the best way to catch a squirrel?
Go climb a tree and make a noise like a nut.

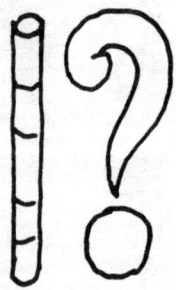

'Why do you have that big hole in your umbrella?'
'So I can look out and see if it's stopped raining, of course.'

Did you eever iver ever in your
  leaf life loaf
See the deevil divil devil kiss
  his weef wife woaf?
No, I neever niver never in my
  leaf life loaf
Saw the deevil divil devil kiss
  his weef wife woaf.

Note: The 'i' in divil, iver, and niver is long, and is pronounced 'eye'.

*Now say each of these
five times, F-A-S-T!*

mixed biscuits
Peggy Babcock
rubber buggy bumpers
black bug's blood
Greek grape leaves

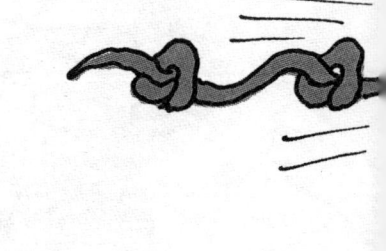

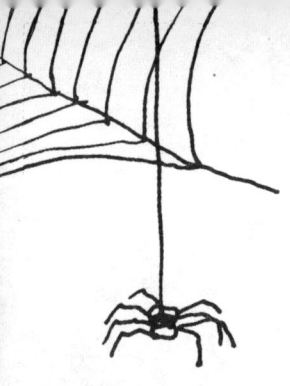

Little Miss Muffet
Sat on a tuffet,
Eating her Irish stew.
Along came a spider
And sat down beside her,
So she ate *him* up, too.

'She told me that you told her the secret I told you not to tell her.'

'Oh, dear! I *told* her not to tell you I told her!'

'Well, goodness, don't tell her that I told you she told me!'

Other Books From The O'Brien Press

THE OWL WHO COULDN'T GIVE A HOOT!
Written and illustrated by Don Conroy
Poor Barny has a big problem – he cannot hoot! But what can his woodland friends do about it? And is it a problem at all?

THE TIGER WHO WAS A ROARING SUCCESS!
Written and illustrated by Don Conroy
The woodland animals are surprised by a strange visitor – a tiger. He wants to return home to India, but how can the animals help to get him there?

CARTOON FUN
Written and illustrated by Don Conroy
How to draw your own cartoons – people, faces, animals, monsters, dinosaurs . . . and more

WILDLIFE FUN
Written and illustrated by Don Conroy
How to draw animals, both realistic and cartoon. Also details and facts about the animals you're drawing.

THAT PEST JONATHAN
William Cole and Illustrated by Tomi Ungerer
Jonathan likes being a pest! And his parents decide they must do something about it. But what can they do? Very little, it seems!

THE DUBLIN ADVENTURE
Siobhán Parkinson
Illustrated by Cathy Henderson
Two children from the country visit Dublin for the first time. What do they make of the big city? It's a strange

place indeed, and very different from the country.

THE COUNTRY ADVENTURE
Siobhán Parkinson
Illustrated by Cathy Henderson
Michelle, a young Dubliner, visits her cousins in the country and finds out about all the strange ways of country living!

THE LEPRECHAUN WHO WISHED HE WASN'T
Siobhán Parkinson
Illustrated by Donald Teskey
Ever hear of a leprechaun who was FED UP with being a leprechaun? Well, Larry is! And he meets Phoebe, who is just FED UP with being too large! A hilarious tale.

THE FIVE HUNDRED
Eilís Dillon
Illustrated by Gareth Floyd
Luca, who lives in Rome, at last gets what he always wanted – a Fiat 500. But it's stolen – and then the excitement begins!

THE KING'S SECRET
Patricia Forde
Illustrated by Donald Teskey
King Lowry Lynch has a *terrible* secret, and no one must find out. The traditional tale in a wacky new style!

YOUR MOVE
Michael Fitzpatrick
Illustrated by Andy Kelly
An exciting chess story in which the pieces come to life and weird things happen! (You learn to play chess too.)

CRAFT
WILDLIFE AT RISK 1 & 2
Elizabeth Sides

Make masks and mobiles of the faces of endangered animals of the world. Learn about their lives, why they are endangered and what is being done to help save them.

BUSY FINGERS 1, 2, 3, 4
Seán C. O'Leary

Great things to make for all the seasons of the year:
1 Spring; 2 Summer; 3 Autumn, Halloween;
4 Christmas, Winter.